Horses!

Horse Care

Trudi Strain Trueit

Cavendish Square
New York

Published in 2014 by Cavendish Square Publishing, LLC
303 Park Avenue South, Suite 1247, New York, NY 10010

First Edition

Library of Congress Cataloging-in-Publication Data
Trueit, Trudi Strain.
Horse Care / Trudi StrainTrueit.
p. cm. — (Horses!)
Includes bibliographical references and index.
Summary: "Provides comprehensive information on the care of horses"—Provided by publisher.
ISBN 978-1-60870-835-2 (hardcover) ISBN 978-1-62712-085-2 (paperback) ISBN 978-1-60870-841-3 (ebook)
1. Horses—Juvenile literature. I. Title.
SF302.T78 2013
636.1'08—dc23
2011023806

Editor: Christine Florie
Art Director: Anahid Hamparian
Series Designer: Virginia Pope

Expert reader: Cathy Herbert, former director of publications, American Horse Shows Association

Photo research by Marybeth Kavanagh

Cover photo by VCL/Taxi/Getty Images

The photographs in this book are used by permission and through the courtesy of: *Alamy*: Ernie Janes, 4; Juniors Bildarchiv, 22, 23, 26; Krista Rossow, 36; *SuperStock*: 15; NaturePL, 7; age fotostock, 10; Jerry Shulman, 16; IndexStock, 25; Cusp, 31; Photononstop, 38; *The Image Works*: Jeff Greenberg, 12; Sorge/Caro/ullstein bild, 29; David R. Frazier, 33; *AP Photo*: Lincoln Journal Star, Eric Gregory, 17; *Photolibrary*: Claudius Thiriet /Peter Arnold, 19; *Getty Images*: Steve Ganem/Workbook Stock, 20; *Newscom*: Uschi Gerschner, 40

Printed in the United States of America

Contents

One

Horse Keeping

It is a crisp, clear morning in April. Fourteen-year-old Julianne is excited to ride her horse, Missy. But first, there's work to do. The **American quarter horse** must be **groomed**. "I like grooming her outside," said Julianne. "She likes it, too. She gets to eat dandelions."

Julianne leads Missy by a **halter** to the pasture. She makes sure the **mare** is safely and securely tied to a tree. Julianne has brought her grooming tools with her from the barn. The wooden box contains several combs and brushes made for horses, along with a **hoof pick**. She begins by brushing Missy's coat. As she works, clouds of dirt and hair rise from the horse's body. Using the hoof pick, Julianne carefully removes dirt and rocks from her horse's feet. Finally, she checks Missy's body and legs for signs of swelling, heat, or injury. "I do this before and after I ride," explained Julianne. "Horses can easily get injured. You have to always be watchful."

← Owning a horse requires taking good care of it. Here a girl grooms her horse.

While Julianne works, Missy dines on grass and dandelions. The quarter horse seems to enjoy being groomed. Most horses do. The brushstrokes make them feel good and horses like being clean. Grooming is also a great way for owner and horse to build a better relationship. Each time Julianne touches Missy she is communicating to her, "you can trust me."

When Julianne is finished grooming, she gently rubs Missy's ears (the mare's favorite spot). "Good girl," Julianne said. She puts the grooming tools in the barn and gets her helmet and **tack**—a saddle, stirrups, and other riding equipment.

Horse Work

Horses are fun to ride and own, but they take a lot of work. A horse must have a safe, comfortable place to live. It requires plenty of fresh water and the right kinds of food in the right quantities. It needs regular grooming, exercise, and health care.

It takes time, money, and energy to keep a horse. Experts say that many first-time horse owners don't plan for this. Some end up giving up their horses within just a few years. "The amount of riding you do is small in comparison to the amount of work involved in caring for a horse," said instructor Carolyn Parker, who has been teaching kids how to ride and work with horses for nearly thirty years. "Most of my students love horses, but it's ones who love *everything* about them, from scooping poo to cleaning

Taking care of a horse includes grooming, providing it with a good shelter, and exercise.

Try Before You Buy

A great way to discover what it's like to have a horse without making a full commitment is to arrange a lease agreement. In a lease, you pay for the care of a horse or split the cost with other people. In return, you get to ride the horse. You may also do some chores, too. This is what Julianne did. For two years, she leased Missy and helped to train her while continuing to take lessons. Recently, Julianne bought Missy. "Leasing is nice because you get to know a horse's personality and make sure you're a good fit," says Julianne. If you decide to lease a horse, be sure to get the rental agreement in writing.

tack, who stick with it. And it's like learning a whole new language."

No one can look after a horse alone. **Equine** (EE-quine) experts are also necessary. Horse owners rely on a team of professionals, such as a veterinarian, an equine dentist, and a **farrier** (a person who shoes horses) to keep their horses healthy. Also, a new horse owner often takes lessons from an instructor to learn how to ride, train, and work with a horse. Many young horse owners choose to join a local riding club or 4-H Youth Development club. These types of clubs allow kids to learn more about horse care in a group setting, meet other horse lovers their own age, and get involved in shows and competitions.

There is more to looking after a horse than providing food and water, shelter, and health care. It also involves keeping a horse happy. Horses are emotional animals. They form connections with the people who care for them, just as Julianne and Missy have done. As you'll learn, horses view the world differently than people do. They have their own way of communicating, too. And anyone, even you, can learn their language.

Clearly, keeping a horse is a big responsibility. But horse owners like Julianne will tell you that the rewards are worth the hard work. "I love having my own horse," she said. "I like the feeling of being able to go anywhere and do whatever I want with Missy. We can ride the trails, or I can just brush her in the pasture while she grazes. I can't imagine not having horses in my life."

Two

A Good Home

One of the most important decisions that horse owners make is where to keep their horses. People with limited outdoor space or busy lifestyles often **board** their animals at a nearby barn. Horse owners with land may choose to keep their horses at home. Backyard care can be fun, because owners get to spend more time with their horses. It's also less expensive than boarding. Yet, it takes more time and carries the greatest risk. Horses can be injured by holes in the pasture, broken fences, or other hazards. A backyard caregiver must always make sure a horse has a safe environment.

Even when people have land, there are plenty of reasons why they might choose to board their horses. First, horses are herd animals. In the wild, they live in groups for socialization and protection (horses are **prey** for some other animals). Without other horses to interact with, a horse may get lonely, bored, or fearful. It helps to have other animals, such as

← Horse owners have to choose where to board their horse. This horse is in his assigned stall in a stable.

In full boarding, horses have access to a pasture or paddock where they can socialize with other horses.

goats, donkeys, or llamas, though horses prefer the company of their own kind. Boredom and stress can lead to behavioral problems such as biting, pawing, pacing, or chewing wood. Boarding is also an excellent choice for a new horse owner. It allows the horse to receive excellent care from professionals while the owner gains experience. Finally, boarding is flexible. Horse owners can do some caretaking themselves or leave it all to others. Here are the most common boarding options:

- Full board: A horse has an assigned stall in a stable. It also has access to a pasture and/or paddock—a fenced outdoor area near the barn where it can rest, eat, exercise, and socialize with other horses. The barn's staff members take care of the horse's needs. They give it food and water. They muck out, or clean, the stall. They provide turnout, meaning they allow the horse to go outdoors to visit the paddock and pasture. For an owner who can't get to the stable every day, this is a good way to go.

- Self-board or partial board: As with full board, a horse has a stall and access to a paddock and/or pasture. However, the horse owner supplies the food, feeds the horse, and does some or all of the chores. Self-board costs less—often about half the amount of full board—but an owner must get to the stable at least twice a day.

Getting On Board

When selecting a boarding facility, try to find a place that's near your home. The grounds and stable should be clean and well maintained. The pasture should be grassy, with few rocks. It should have an arena (preferably roofed) where you can exercise your horse. If you are a new horse owner, look for a facility that offers professional instruction, too.

- Pasture board: A horse remains outside in a fenced pasture year-round. It usually has a three-sided, roofed shelter called a run-in. The barn may supply food and water, but sometimes the owner must provide them. Pasture board is the least expensive boarding option. Owners should make arrangements for a pasture-boarded horse to have a stall if it is sick or injured and during severe weather.

In all of these boarding options, the owner is typically responsible for **working**, or exercising, the horse and arranging veterinary care. The boarding facility usually provides vitamins, deworming medication, and blankets.

Pasture Matters

A horse's first love is **grazing**. Horses are **herbivores**, meaning that grass and plants are their main sources of nutrition. No matter where a horse lives—in a backyard or at a barn—it wants access to a field. A pasture provides several necessities for its well-being:

- grasses and plants to eat
- space to play, run, and rest
- trees for shade
- freedom to see or socialize with other horses, animals, and people

Horses need a lot of space to graze and roam.

How much land does a horse require? Experts recommend at least an acre. More property may be necessary, however, depending on soil and weather conditions and how often the horse is turned out. A boarding facility that takes care of many horses will likely have many acres of land.

To keep the grass healthy for grazing, a pasture must be mowed, watered, and fertilized regularly. It must also be kept clean. Once a day or every few days, the horse's **manure** is scooped and piled away from the pasture. The manure may be trucked from the property, sold to farmers or gardeners, or left to **compost**.

Ideally, someone walks the paddock and pasture to check for hazards before turning out the horse. These areas must be free of holes, sharp rocks, trash, farm equipment, poisonous plants, and anything that might injure

To keep horses safe, their pastures are fenced in.

a horse. At a boarding barn, a **stable hand** does this chore. At home, it falls to the horse owner to inspect the backyard pasture for hazards.

A pasture is fenced to keep horses from wandering into areas where they don't belong or getting close to hazards. Fencing is constructed from wood, plastic (with low-voltage electricity), or wire designed for use with horses. Fences do not contain barbed wire, because it can injure a horse. The best pastures are mostly flat and have good drainage. They do not have sections with standing water or deep mud. A horse that lives or works in continually muddy conditions could get injured. It is also at risk for thrush, a foot fungus, and mud fever, a skin infection.

A Stable Home

It may seem unkind to leave a horse outdoors all the time, but most horses are quite content living outside. In the wild, they have adapted to survive in all but the coldest of earth's environments. Still, many owners prefer to keep their horses in a stable at night for safety. Stabling can also make older horses or those with special needs more comfortable.

A stabled horse has its own stall.

Every stabled horse has its own stall. Stable walls are typically made of wood, metal, cement block, or metal mesh. These materials can stand up to the kicking, chewing, and other wear horses put on them. Many front walls have grills made of bars. This creates good airflow and allows the horse to see out. Many stalls have a sliding wooden window in the back to give the horse another view to the outdoors. Some people attach mirrors to the wall so a horse can see its reflection. The mirrors are made of polished stainless steel and framed in wood (glass is not used because it could injure a horse). Caretakers may add toys, such as balls or traffic cones, to keep the horse from being bored.

Good drainage in a stall is crucial. A single horse may produce up to 50 pounds of manure and 10 gallons of urine every day! This is why the flooring in a stall is smooth, flat, and easy to clean. Dirt, clay, or rubber mats offer cushioning for a horse's legs. On top, the bedding should be absorbent, dust-free, nontoxic, comfortable, and easy to care for. Wood shavings or

Time for Chores

If you are a new horse owner and are doing most of the work yourself, make a copy of the horse care checklist below. Keep it handy until you've memorized your chores.

Horse Care Checklist

Every day:

- ✓ feed horse two to three times
- ✓ provide fresh water two to three times
- ✓ check paddock and pasture for hazards
- ✓ turn out
- ✓ groom horse (before and after riding)
- ✓ ride horse
- ✓ muck out stall

chips and wood or straw pellets are all smart bedding choices.

Each day, a horse's stall must be mucked out. These are the supplies needed to muck out a stall:

- wheelbarrow
- pitchfork (designed for the type of bedding being used)
- broom

A horse is usually removed from the stall before it's cleaned. However, some horses remain in their stalls. They have learned to stand aside during the cleaning process. Placing the wheelbarrow near the stall door blocks the entrance so the horse cannot escape. A steel or plastic fork is used to sift through the bedding and pick up all the manure, which is placed in the wheelbarrow. Urine spots in the bedding are also removed with the pitchfork and put in the wheelbarrow. Next, the remaining bedding is swept against the wall with the broom or fork. When the floor is dry, the bedding is raked back into place. Fresh bedding is added. The stall is now clean.

The manure from the wheelbarrow is dumped into a pile outside the barn. Experts recommend completely mucking out a stall about once a week by replacing all of the old bedding with new bedding. This routine may seem like a lot to remember, but it doesn't take long to learn. A tidy stall helps a horse stay clean, comfortable, and healthy.

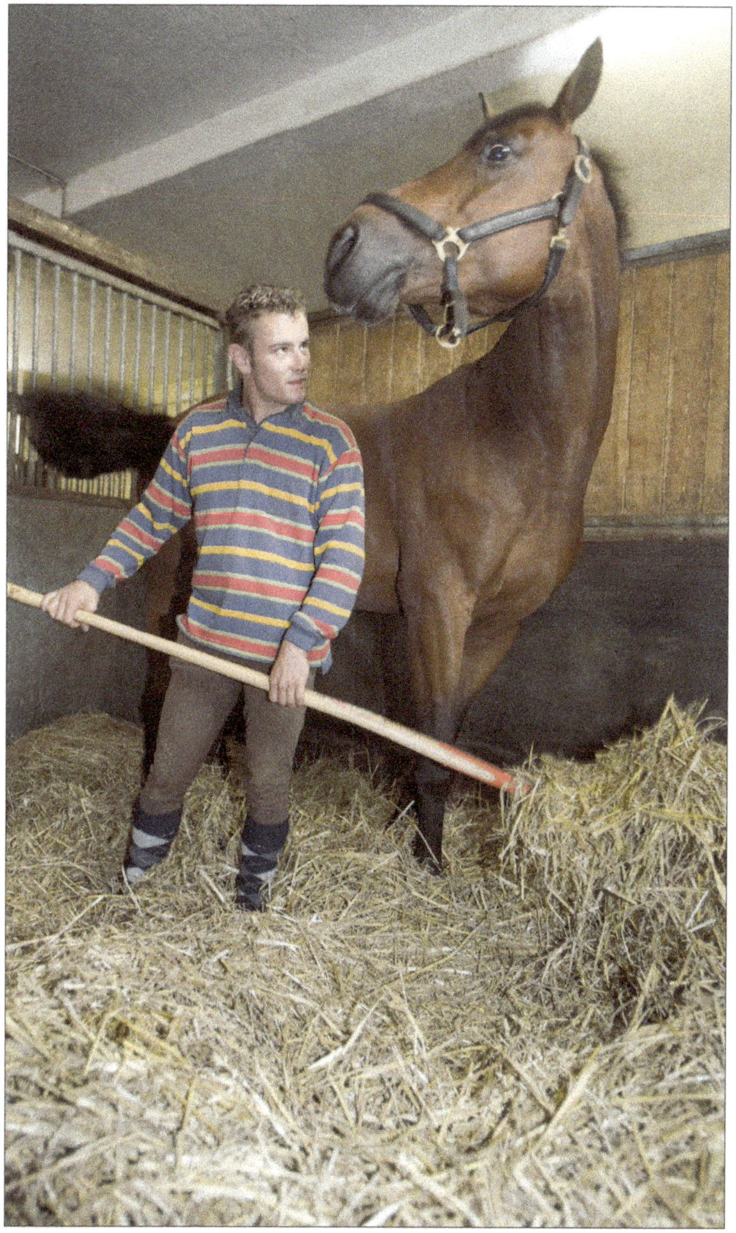

This horse has been taught to stand aside while its stall is being cleaned.

Three

Eating Right

If you've ever watched horses in a pasture, you know they spend a lot of time munching on grass. Horses are grazers. Bermuda grass, bromegrass, bluegrass, timothy, and orchard grass are among their favorite **forage**. Many horses also enjoy dandelions, a weed that is rich in minerals, such as calcium and magnesium.

Not all plants are safe for horses to eat, however. Many plants commonly found in backyards can harm horses. These include yew, rhododendron, foxglove, delphinium, and bracken fern. Black locust, red maple, cherry, and oak (as well as their acorns) are among the trees horses should not eat. Most poisonous plants cause only minor stomach problems, but some may do permanent damage or even kill a horse. However, horses instinctively avoid plants that aren't good for them, unless they are very hungry or no good grass is available.

← This horse grazes on fresh grass.

Hey, Hay!

It would be perfect if horses could get all their nutrients from grazing, but it would take 28 acres of pastureland to provide fresh forage for just a single horse! So, along with grass, most horse owners also feed their horses hay, or dried grasses and plants. Hay is a great source of fiber and helps with digestion. It also satisfies a horse's natural desire to chew.

Hay should be leafy, green, and fresh smelling. If it's brown, dusty, moldy, or musty smelling, it is not used. Hay is checked for sand, sticks, poisonous plants, netting, and other hazardous items before being fed to a horse. Horses are fed from a hay feeder to be sure that dirt and sand aren't mixed with their food. Hay is stored in a cool, dry place off the ground so it won't get dirty or moldy.

Hay provides a good source of fiber and nutrition for horses. It should always be clean and fresh.

Many owners also give their horses grains, such as oats, corn, and barley. Grains provide extra energy and give a horse variety in her diet. A horse's breed, age, activity level, and health issues determine the type and amount of food provided.

Horses have small stomachs and are unable to digest large amounts of food at one time. So stabled horses are usually fed two or three times a day, with meals spaced evenly apart. Generally, horses eat about 2 percent of

Pass the Salt

When horses exercise, they lose salt through their sweat just like people do. Salt is essential to a horse's diet. Without enough salt, a horse may lose its appetite resulting in weight loss. Horses instinctively know they require salt and will seek it out as they need it. This is why salt and mineral blocks made especially for horses should always be available in the pasture, paddock, and stall for a horse to lick as it pleases.

their body weight each day, so a 1,000-pound horse would typically require about 20 pounds of food per day.

Most horses enjoy a snack now and then. Healthy treats such as apples, carrots, and pears are excellent choices. However, some foods that humans eat are harmful to horses, such as cabbage, potatoes, tomatoes, broccoli, onions, and rhubarb. Fruits and vegetables should be cut into small pieces before feeding to keep the horse from choking. Also, it's wise to put treats in a bucket rather than hand-feed, so a horse doesn't mistake a finger for a snack.

Thirsty Creatures

A horse drinks about 10 gallons of water every day, so clean, fresh water must always be available everywhere she spends time. **Troughs** (TRAWFS) must be emptied, cleaned, and refilled with fresh water at least once a day. In an area with harsh winters, an insulated water trough is a helpful option. Many horse owners use an automatic watering system that offers horses a constant supply of fresh water (though they must keep alert for frozen pipes in the winter).

Horses drink more water in hot weather or after working. They drink less in cold weather or when they are ill. How can you tell if a horse is getting enough water? Using your thumb and index finger, pick up a fold of skin in the horse's neck or shoulder area. Pull the skin slightly away from the body, and then release it. In a well-hydrated horse, the skin will snap back within a few seconds. If the skin remains puckered for more than five seconds, the horse is likely dehydrated. It's time to call the vet.

Now that you've learned some of the basics of caring for a horse, read on to discover more about how to keep it looking and feeling its best.

Horses drink a lot! It's vital that clean, fresh water always be available.

Four

A Healthy Horse

Did you know that the average horse lives to be about twenty-five years old? Regular exercise, grooming, and health care can go a long way toward helping a horse live a long, active life.

Horses like to run, play, and be ridden. A horse should get thirty to sixty minutes of moderate exercise five days a week. A horse that doesn't get enough exercise or has sudden changes in its exercise routine is at risk for digestive, leg, and hoof problems. At the end of a ride, if a horse is breathing hard or sweating, it must be cooled. An owner does this by walking her around the stable for five to ten minutes. Sips of water are okay after exercise, but a horse should not eat food until it has cooled completely. A horse is cool when the sweat has dried on its body and its breathing has returned to normal. Giving a horse food before it has cooled down can cause digestive problems.

← With proper care, horses can live a long, happy, and healthy life.

Clean and Shiny

Most horses like being touched, as long as it's done *their* way. They prefer being rubbed on the ears, forehead, neck, and **withers**. They don't enjoy being tickled or slapped. Horses usually enjoy the grooming process. In the pasture, you'll often see one horse using its teeth to groom another's withers. Grooming accomplishes several things. It keeps a horse clean and comfortable. It allows an owner to spot health issues early. Finally, it's a great way for horse and owner to bond. A horse needs to be groomed once a day, or twice on the days it is ridden (before and after exercise). Here are the basic tools used in grooming a horse:

- rubber currycomb
- dandy brush (stiff brush)
- body brush (soft brush)
- sponge
- mane comb (plastic)
- hoof pick with brush
- towel or polishing cloth

Before grooming, the horse must be safely and securely tied to a solid object, such as a post. It's best to begin at the top of the neck on one side of the horse and work toward the rear, then switch sides and repeat.

First, using the currycomb, the coat is rubbed in a firm, circular motion

Grooming keeps a horse clean and happy.

to work any dirt loose. The groomer (which will likely be the rider or owner) must be gentle around bony areas like the back and withers and must not curry the face or below the knees. Next, the stiff dandy is used to whisk away the dirt that's been loosened. Again, a groomer begins at the top of the horse's neck, works down one side of the body, and then moves to the other side. This time, short, sweeping strokes are used. Dust and hair rise from the coat.

The dandy brush is gently used to remove dirt from below the knees. Mud on the legs its left to dry and then brushed away with the dandy brush. To remove fine dirt, the groomer picks up the soft body brush and uses light, short strokes. The horse's coat gets shinier. Next, the tail is smoothed with the dandy brush. A mane comb is gently run through the mane to remove tangles. The face and head are cleaned with a soft towel. If there is dirt near the eyes, it is carefully removed with a damp sponge.

Now, it's time to clean the horse's feet. Facing the rear of a horse, the groomer carefully lifts the horse's foot. Using the hoof pick, she scrapes downward to remove manure, rocks, and dirt from the underside of the hoof and around the inside edge of the horseshoe. A groomer is always careful not to touch the **frog**—the delicate, fleshy pad at the back center of the hoof. Dirt is swept away with the hoof brush. Finally, the horse's body is wiped down with a soft towel or polishing cloth.

Many people do additional grooming, too. They might use a shedding blade to remove hair, apply hoof dressing (to keep the feet from cracking), or wipe on natural insecticide (to keep flies away). Now and then, a horse can benefit from a bath. The temperature of the bath water should be above 65 degrees Fahrenheit to make sure it doesn't get chilled. After a summer ride, it's the perfect time for a cool bath!

Raising the Hoof

To pick up a horse's foot, stand beside the horse and face the rear. Slip your hand down the leg, past the knee, to just above the **fetlock**. Now, gently squeeze, pressing upward. The horse should pick up her foot. Cradle the horse's foot in one hand while you use the other hand to clean with the hoof pick. Have an adult help you until you feel confident doing it on your own. You don't want to injure your horse or yourself.

An Ounce of Prevention

It's no wonder we tend to think of horses as big, powerful animals. **Draft horses** may measure up to 19 **hands** (72 inches)! Even so, when it comes to their health, horses can be fragile. What may first appear to be a small injury or infection can become serious if left untreated.

Every day, a horse should be given a full body check. After grooming, the owner runs her hands over the horse's body. She will feel for bumps,

Tummy Troubles

Each year, about one in ten horses will suffer from **colic**, a disorder of the digestive system. Colic may be as harmless as a little gas or as serious as a blockage in the intestines. It is the number one killer of horses. Bad hay, sand in the hay, poisonous plants, sudden dietary changes, overeating, or inadequate worming can lead to colic. To prevent colic, never work a horse right after it has eaten or feed her after it has been worked. Stick to a regular feeding schedule, and always have clean water available. Also, inspect all hay. Symptoms of colic include pawing the ground, pacing, repeated rolling, sudden sweating, lack of appetite, and looking at or kicking the belly.

swelling, or hot spots (heat can signal infection). It's also important to look for scabs, hair loss, and discharge from the nose or eyes. Are there any cracks, nicks, bumps, or bruises on the tops or bottoms of the hooves? Is a hoof overgrown or a shoe missing? Does the hoof smell bad (a sign of infection)? The owner must keep alert for limping, lack of appetite, depression, or sleepiness. Is the horse sensitive to the touch? Does it seem uncomfortable or in pain? If the horse has any changes in behavior or physical health, a vet should be contacted.

Just like humans, horses need to have their teeth checked. Unlike us, however, a horse's teeth continue to grow throughout her lifetime. Along with doing a full mouth exam, the vet or equine dentist will file down sharp teeth in a process called **floating**. Floating should be done once a year for adult horses and twice a year for younger and older horses.

A veterinarian checks the health of a horse's teeth.

Vital Stats

It's a good idea to have all of your horse's important information in one place, especially in an emergency. Make a copy of the form below, fill it in, and keep the records handy. Update it once a year.

My Horse's Information

Today's Date: ______________________________

Horse's Name: ______________________________

Breed: ______________________________

Color: ______________________________

Height: ______________________________

Weight: ______________________________

Age: ______________________________

Veterinarian: ______________________________

Vet's Phone Number: ______________________________

Vet's Emergency Number: ______________________________

A horse also has several yearly appointments with a farrier. A horse's hooves grow a quarter of an inch per month. About every two months, the farrier will visit the boarding facility or backyard pasture. During this painless procedure, he or she will trim the horses' hooves and replace shoes as needed.

A horse, typically, gets a yearly exam from its veterinarian. The veterinarian may check the horse's temperature, heart rate, and weight. There are a couple of ways to check a horse's weight. One way is to place the animal on a livestock scale. This method gives the most accurate reading, but not everyone has such a large scale handy. An easier and quicker way to calculate weight is by placing a height-weight measuring tape around a horse's midsection. It is important for a horse owner to always know a horse's weight so food and medication may be given in proper amounts. The veterinarian inspects the horse to make sure it is in good condition. A horse in ideal shape will have a back that is level or slightly creased. The ribs will not be seen, but can be easily felt. The withers will be rounded, with the shoulders and neck blending smoothly into the body. The veterinarian will also place the horse on a regular schedule for vaccinations and de-worming.

Horse owners should not be afraid to call their veterinarian when they have questions or concerns about horse care. Most veterinarians are happy to offer advice or examine a horse, if necessary. Their goal is the same as every horse owner's: to keep a horse in top shape!

Five

A Happy Horse

You've probably heard the term *horse whisperer*. It's used to refer to someone who has a special knack for communicating with horses. In truth, it isn't a gift or a mysterious secret at all. Anyone can learn to be a horse whisperer—even you!

Horse Sense

Horses are clever, curious, and sensitive. They are ruled by natural instinct, and the social group is important to them. They are also prey for other animals, such as wolves and cougars. A horse's view of the world is guided by its desire to fit in to the group and its fear of predators. Keeping these two traits in mind can help an owner better understand a horse's behavior and communicate with it.

← Communication between a horse and its owner is important for the upkeep and happiness of the horse.

In any herd, there is a pecking order of leaders and followers. For a horse to obey a human, it needs to believe its owner is higher in the pecking order than it is. This isn't as difficult as you might think. "When you take charge it actually makes your horse feel more comfortable," explained Julianne, the young horse owner from the beginning of this book. "Horses are constantly looking around to see who is the leader, so by staying calm and in control you are taking the pressure off them to lead." A horse owner must be the leader in everything she does with the horse, from feeding to grooming to riding. A horse learns from every interaction it has with its owner, so being consistent is important. Sometimes a horse will want to be at the top of the pecking order. Perhaps it takes a carrot before it is offered to it. Usually, saying "No" in a firm voice will remind it who is the leader. There are times when a horse may not understand what it is being asked to do. Patience is key. A rider must take a deep breath and start again—or try a different approach.

A horse owner must establish the "leader" role in her relationship with her horse.

Taking lessons from a professional instructor can help an owner form a bond, respect, and trust with her horse.

Trust is critical, because horses are timid. It's in their nature to always be watching for predators. They run from anything they consider a threat. Horses hate surprises. Objects or people that move quickly or make an unexpected or unfamiliar noise may **spook** them. This includes plastic bags flying in the wind, bicycles, cars, airplanes, radios, or even someone waving his arms. Horses have an excellent memory, too. They can recall cues up to a year after they've learned them. They remember bad experiences as well as good ones. Frightening memories can haunt a horse and hamper training. If a horse has a particular fear, a trainer is often called in to help it overcome it.

Beware of the Kick Zone

You can spook a horse by standing where it can't see you. With eyes on the sides of its head, a horse has a wide field of vision to each side. But it does have blind spots, or places it can't see, such as right under its nose, on the back near its withers, and directly behind its tail. This area in the rear is known as the kick zone, because a startled horse is likely to kick out at anything it senses but cannot see. Always stand to the side of a horse and watch your feet so you don't get stepped on.

Body Language

This horse is happy in its stall, yet also curious about the camera and photographer.

Is a horse swishing its tail or stomping a front foot? It may be saying that it is bored, annoyed, or just bothered by flies. A horse's body can reveal a lot about what's going on in its mind. A horse that's content will have its head and neck in an attentive but not stiff position, eyes partially closed, and both ears relaxed or tipped to the side. In contrast, a fearful horse will lift its head and neck high, open its eyes wide, and point both ears in the direction of the danger.

Horses get bored quickly, so it's important for an owner to give her horse some fun activities to do. Take it on a different trail, teach it a new skill, ride bareback, or give it toys to play with (most horses love traffic cones). "If Missy is doing the same thing for too long, she'll pretend to be lazy," said Julianne. "I try to make working fun for her. I might set up some cones and we'll do a pattern, or we'll jump. She loves jumping."

Read My Ears

Are you looking to quickly gauge a horse's mood? Watch its ears. Ears that are pricked forward mean a horse is alert and listening. A horse that's being ridden may have one ear cocked forward and one ear turned backward to keep track of what's happening around it while staying attentive to its rider. Beware of ears that are flattened or pinned back. This signals resistance or anger.

Hooked on Horses

When it comes to looking after a horse, there is always more to learn! Even experienced horse owners read books, take classes, and talk with other owners to improve their methods of horse care. If you are interested in learning how to care for a horse, take classes at a local stable or riding school. You may also want to join a club, like your local branch of 4-H. Being part of a club allows you to gain hands-on experience, meet other horse owners your age, and get involved in shows and competitions. Use the resources in the Find Out More section on page 44 to get started.

If you are fortunate enough to lease or own a horse, give it the best care you can. Give it training, exercise, and fun. Give it attention and take the time to learn its language. In return, you will have a strong, beautiful, confident horse. Best of all, you will have a friend forever.

Glossary

American quarter horse A compact, muscular horse originally bred for speed.

board To provide a horse with food, water, and a place to live.

colic A painful and possibly deadly digestive disorder in horses.

compost To decay in order to be used as fertilizer.

draft horses Large horses bred for heavy tasks, such as farming.

equine Pertaining to horses.

farrier A professional who trims and shoes horses' hooves.

fetlock A horse's ankle joint.

floating Filing a horse's teeth.

forage The grasses and plants that horses eat.

frog The triangular, fleshy pad on the bottom of a horse's hoof.

grazing Eating small meals frequently throughout the day.

groomed Cleaned and brushed.

halter A harness that fits over a horse's head that is used to lead or secure the animal.

hands Units used to measure horses; 1 hand equals 4 inches.

herbivores Animals that feed on only plants.

hoof pick A metal tool with a hook used to clean horse's hooves.

manure Solid animal waste often used as fertilizer.

mare A female horse over four years old.

prey An animal that is hunted and eaten by other animals.

spook To frighten something suddenly.

stable hand A professional who helps to care for horses at a barn.

tack The equipment used to ride a horse.

troughs Large tubs for holding food or water.

withers The bump between a horses's shoulder blades at the base of the neck.

working Exercising, riding, or training a horse.

Find Out More

Books

Bird, Jo. *Horse Care and Fitness: The Young Rider's Handbook*. Neptune City, NJ: T.F.H. Publications, 2009.

Mack, Gail. *Horses*. New York: Marshall Cavendish Benchmark, 2010.

Niven, Felicia Lowenstein. *Learning to Care for a Horse*. Berkeley Heights, NJ: Enslow, 2011.

Vogel, Colin. *Complete Horse Care Manual*. New York: Dorling Kindersley, 2011.

Websites

4-H Youth Development

www.4-h.org

4-H Youth Development is sponsored by the U.S. Department of Agriculture and organized through your local university's Cooperative Extension Office. 4-H clubs can connect you with professional trainers and other horse owners your age. Log on to the website to find a Cooperative Extension Office that organizes 4-H clubs in your area.

American Association of Equine Practitioners (AAEP)

www.aaep.org

Here you can read articles about horse health, sign up for a horse owner e-newsletter, and find an AAEP-certified veterinarian in your area. Have a question about your horse's health? Just click on "Ask the Vet."

American Society for the Prevention of Cruelty to Animals (ASPCA)

www.aspca.org/pet-care/horse-care

This is a great site for kids to learn about general horse care, such as nutrition, toxic plants, hoof care, training, and more. Click on the virtual pet behaviorist for solutions regarding various behavioral issues. For help with a specific problem, go to "Ask the Experts." The ASPCA also operates a twenty-four–hour poison center hotline for horse owners who fear their horse may have eaten a harmful plant.

Index

Page numbers in **boldface** are illustrations.

About the Author

Trudi Strain Trueit is the author of more than eighty fiction and nonfiction books for kids. A former television weather forecaster, she especially enjoys writing about nature and animals. Her titles include the Backyard Safari series and Creepy Critters rebus series. She lives near Seattle, Washington, with her husband, Bill, a photography teacher and freelance photographer. Visit www.truditrueit.com to learn more.